ADAPTING FOR SURVIVAL

SKIN

WRITTEN BY STEPHEN SAVAGE

Wayland

ADAPTING FOR SURVIVAL

Titles in the series

• EYES   • EARS   • NOSES   • MOUTHS
• SKIN   • HANDS AND FEET

Front cover: Girls with rabbits, a chameleon lizard

Title page: A leopard

Series editor: Francesca Motisi
Book editor: Jannet King
Designer: Jean Wheeler
Production Controller: Nancy Pitcher

First published in 1995 by
Wayland (Publishers) Ltd
61 Western Road, Hove
East Sussex BN3 1JD, England

British Library Cataloguing in Publication Data
Savage, Stephen
Skin. – (Adapting for Survival Series)
I. Title II. Series
591.5

ISBN 0-7502-1588-7

Printed and bound in Italy by
L.E.G.O. S.p.A., Vicenza

Typeset by Jean Wheeler

Picture acknowledgements
The publishers would like to thank the following for allowing their photographs to be reproduced in this book: Bruce Coleman Limited: 7 (top/Gerald Cubitt) (bottom/Jeff Foott), 9 (Hans Reinhard), 10 (Kim Taylor), 12 (bottom/Gary Retherford), 13 (top/Frans Lanting), 14 (Jane Burton), 15 (top/John Cancalosi) (bottom/Jane Burton), 18 (bottom/John Cancalosi), 19 (top/Jane Burton) (bottom/Andrew J Purcell), 23 (top/Erwin & Peggy Bauer), 24 (bottom/Hector Rivarola), 25 (top/Luiz Claudio Marigo) (bottom/M P L Fogden), 26 (bottom/Brian J Coates), 28 (bottom/Jane Burton), 29 (Kim Taylor); Cephas: 18 (top/Dorothy Burrows); Natural History Photographic Agency: cover (bottom/Gerard Lacz), 16 (Anthony Bannister), 21 (bottom/Jenry Ausloos), 23 (bottom/Stephen Dalton); Oxford Scientific Films: title page (David W Breed), 4 (top/G I Bernard), 8 (Michael Leach), 11 (top/James H Robinson) (bottom/Stan Osolinski), 12 (top/Z Lesczynski), 13 (bottom/Max Gibbs), 17 (top/Howard Hall) (bottom/Pam & Willy Kemp), 20 (Doug Allan), 21 (top/David B Fleetham), 24 (top/Leonard Lee Rue), 26 (top/Andrew Plumptre), 28 (top/Zig Lesczynski); Tony Stone Worldwide: 5 (top/Sue Ann Miller); Wayland: cover (top), 5 (bottom), 27 (top); ZEFA: 6 (Liedermooy), 22 (Will & Demi McIntyre), 27 (bottom/John Flowerdew). The artwork on pages 4 and 31 is by Peter Bull.

Contents

Human skin

One square centimetre of human skin contains approximately ten hairs, one metre of blood vessels, one hundred sweat glands and millions of skin cells. It also contains numerous sense cells that send messages to our brain about the things we touch.

The human body is completely covered by skin. This skin is made up of many layers of skin cells and is the body's largest organ. The top layer of skin is made from dead cells and helps protect us from dirt and harmful bacteria.

A layer of cells near the surface of the skin reacts to the harmful rays of the sun by producing a protective pigment (colour). This can cause our skin to form freckles, or if we stay out in the strong sun for too long, our skin can become sunburnt. When skin is sunburnt it becomes red and sore.

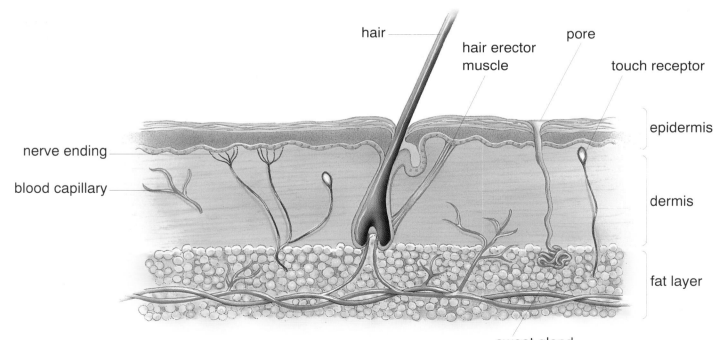

A baby's skin is soft and stretchy. As people get older their skin becomes drier and loses its elasticity, causing it to wrinkle.

This damaged skin peels off after a few days but if you become sunburnt often, you may do permanent damage to your skin. The sun is at its strongest at the Equator. People living in the areas of the world nearest to the Equator (or those whose ancestors did) have dark skin. This adaptation partly protects them from the harmful rays of the sun.

The skin is also a sense organ, providing us with a sense of touch. There are many special cells in the skin. Some are sensitive to cold, heat or pain. Some of our skin has changed slightly in its structure to make hair and nails. As you will see in the rest of this book, a fish's scales, a cat's fur, a bird's feathers and a tortoise's shell are also made from special skin cells.

Our skin contains sense cells that enable us to feel with the whole of our body. This boy is enjoying the softness of the rabbit's fur against his skin.

Thick skin

Human skin is quite thin and easily damaged. If we cut or graze ourself, special pain cells tell us that we have damaged our skin and need treatment. The damaged area can be covered with a plaster to stop dirt and bacteria getting into the wound while new skin cells grow.

Some animals, such as rhinoceroses and elephants, have very thick skin. This protects them against injury from predators and other animals of the same species. The skin of an elephant can be as much as 25 mm thick on some parts of its body.

Even a thick-skinned elephant can find a mosquito's bite troublesome. This one is trying to protect its skin from bites by covering iself in mud.

The horn of the rhinoceros is actually made from a special skin. The cells are so tightly packed that the horn is extremely hard. The rhinoceros uses its horn to defend itself against predators and in fights with other rhinos.

Seals and sea lions come ashore on beaches to have their pups. A male seal or sea lion will defend an area of beach from other males by fighting them off. They use their sharp teeth as weapons, biting each other's neck, if they get the chance. The skin and fat (blubber) around their neck is much thicker than on other parts of the body. This means that they rarely do any serious damage to each other.

The thick layer of skin and blubber (fat) around this male sea lion's neck protects it from bites in battles with other sea lions.

Hair and fur

Although all mammals are covered in skin, most are also covered in hair or fur for extra protection. Animals that are covered in hair include horses, monkeys and apes. Humans are also covered in hair, which varies in thickness and length depending on the part of the body. Only on the palms of our hands and the soles of our feet are we totally hairless.

Other animals, such as cats of all sizes, rabbits and mice, are covered in fur. This is similar to hair, but much finer and softer. Both hair and fur keep the animal warm. It is only humans that need to wear clothes for warmth.

A chinchilla has perhaps the softest fur of all mammals.

Some of the clothes we wear are made from the hair of animals. Sheep, for example, have thick, hairy coats which can be cut off and turned into wool thread. This is done by a process known as spinning. The wool thread is used to make all kinds of clothes and blankets.

An animal's hair or fur is moulted throughout its life. Most furry or hairy animals will 'change their coat' according to the season, growing thicker coats for the winter, which they then shed in the Spring.

Some animals, including cats, mice and moles, have thick hairs, called whiskers, on their head and face. The whiskers are connected at their roots to sensitive cells so that the animals can feel if the whiskers touch anything. This is very useful when they are finding their way around in the dark.

Some mammals, such as mice, squirrels and rabbits, are born bald and grow fur after a few days. This mother rabbit has pulled out some of her own fur to keep her newborn babies warm.

The sensitive whiskers on a rabbit's face help it to find its way through the network of dark tunnels in which it lives.

Feathers

The body of a bird is covered in feathers. Like hair and fur, this body covering grows from the skin and helps to keep the bird warm. The feathers that give each bird its typical shape are called 'contour feathers'. Underneath these is a layer of soft, downy feathers. Female ducks actually pull out some of these feathers to line their nest. Baby birds often have downy feathers before their adult feathers grow.

A bird's feathers must be kept in good condition and much of their time is taken up with preening and bathing. Birds lose their feathers (moult) once a year.

The feathers on a bird's wings are called 'flight feathers'. These allow birds to travel great distances to find food or escape from danger. An owl has very soft flight feathers so that it can silently swoop down on its prey. A bird's tail feathers are used to help it balance when flying or sitting on a branch.

Birds use their feathers to blend in with their surroundings. The female mallard duck, for example, is a dull brown so that she can sit on her nest and not be seen. But, like mammals, birds also use their feathers to give out signals to other birds – either to attract them or to warn them away.

▲ The cormorant's feathers are not waterproof and tend to become waterlogged when it swims. This makes the cormorant heavy in the water so that it can stay beneath the surface for a long time, searching for fish. It has to spend a lot of time drying itself in the sun and wind.

The feathers of a penguin (and of many other water birds) are 'waterproof'. This means that they do not absorb water. In fact, the penguin's feathers trap a layer of air next to the body, which helps it to bob back up to the surface after diving for fish.

11

Scales

Many creatures have a body covered in scales. These scales can be large and thick enough to protect the animal against attack, or so small that the animal feels smooth and soft to the touch. Some lizards have skin that is hard and spiky, while others have softer skin like that of a snake. Many people think that snakes are cold and slimy but in fact their skin is warm and dry. Snakes move by pushing themselves along the ground with the large scales on the underside of their body.

▲ *If a snake was smooth all over it would be very difficult for it to move along. The large scales on its underside help it to push itself along the ground.*

Scales can be found in surprising places. The coloured patterns on a butterfly's wings are made from thousands of tiny scales.

The shell of this giant tortoise is actually made from extremely hard skin cells.

Animals that use their scales for protection include the tortoise, whose body is covered in hard scales that form a shell. Its legs and head are covered in tough, scaly skin, like that on crocodiles and alligators.

The bodies of most types of fish are covered in protective scales. Fish feel slimy because of a special thick mucus that covers the body. This helps them glide through the water and also helps to protect them from infection. Like mammals and birds, the colour and pattern on their body covering can be used for camouflage or for display.

The scales on the body of this cichlid overlap, like tiles on a roof.

Spiny bodies

Spikes and spines are a good way of protecting the body. Hedgehogs and porcupines use their sharp spines to defend themselves against attack. When approached by an attacker, the porcupine sticks up the spines on its back and tail. If this does not frighten off its attacker, the porcupine rushes backwards, ramming its spikes (known as 'quills') into its enemy. When threatened, the European hedgehog curls itself into a tight, prickly ball.

The European hedgehog rolls itself into a tight ball to put off predators. This one, feeling itself to be out of danger, is just beginning to unroll.

When threatened, the Australian echidna sticks up its sharp spines.

Sea urchins belong to a group of animals called echinoderms, which means 'spiny-skinned'. A sea urchin's body is covered in long spines which protect these slow-moving animals. The spines of some types of sea urchin are poisonous.

When it feels itself to be in danger, a pufferfish blows itself up. This causes its spikes (which usually lie flat against its body) to stick out, and makes it an unappetizing mouthful.

Many fish have spines on their fins and gill covers, but some fish have other defensive spines. The three-spined stickleback has spines on its back which it sticks up when attacked, making this fish hard for other fish to swallow.

Living shells

This giant African land snail is the largest shelled creature on land.

One way of protecting the body is to live inside a hard shell. There are many animals that do this. Some have a single shell (such as a snail); others have a shell made up of two halves (such as a mussel). Unlike the shell of a tortoise, the shells of animals such as snails and mussels are not made from skin cells. They are formed by a thick liquid which oozes out of the animal's body and then hardens.

Animals with one shell are able to move around by carrying their shell on their back. Only a few live on land, the largest being the giant African land snail. Most snails live in ponds, rivers or oceans.

The shells of sea snails may be spiral shaped, smooth or spiky, and some are brightly coloured. Many, like the winkle, feed by scraping tiny seaweeds and algae off the rocks. Others, such as the dogwhelk, can actually attack and eat a mussel by drilling a hole through its shell.

There are many creatures that have two halves to their shells. These tend to stay in one place absorbing food from their surroundings, but most are able to move a short distance to escape from danger or find a better place to feed. Mussels attach themselves to rocks using sticky threads; piddocks actually bore into rock for extra protection. Oysters and scallops lie on the sea-bed, while the razor shell hides beneath the sand.

▲ *The giant clam can grow to a size of one metre across and can weigh 180 kilogrammes.*

Sea shells, like this cowrie, have been used as ornaments and jewellery. In some Pacific Islands, cowrie shells have even been used as money.

Armour

Humans have had to use artificial ways of protecting their soft skin when fighting. Suits of armour like these were worn hundreds of years ago. The overlapping plates on the arms are similar to those on the body of the armadillo.

A shell provides good protection against predators, but it makes it difficult to move around. Some animals, such as insects, spiders, crabs and lobsters, have armoured bodies instead. The armour consists of a tough skin that is jointed, allowing the animal to walk or run. In fact, as these animals have no bones inside their flesh, this outer shell is more than just a body covering; it is a kind of outside skeleton.

Safe inside its protective armour, a crab can move around in search of food or to avoid danger. Crabs have large, armoured pincers that they use when feeding or when defending themselves.

A nine-banded armadillo. The narrow overlapping bands of armour make it more flexible than, say, a tortoise, with its rigid shell.

A hermit crab only has armoured skin on its limbs and part of its body. It protects the rest of its body by living in an empty sea shell, which it carries around on its back. This land hermit crab lives in South-East Asia.

A crab's shell often blends in with its surroundings, as is the case with the adult shore crab, which has a green body for hiding in seaweed-covered tidal pools. Spider crabs have hooks on their back on to which they attach seaweed.

Insects have a firm outer skin that supports and protects their body. Although the skin is not as tough as a crab's, it does help protect them against attack from other small creatures. Some beetles have hard, shiny wing cases that look rather like shells.

Like other beetles, the ladybird has hard wing cases that cover most of its body.

Water mammals

Although our skin is waterproof, we are not really adapted to live in the water. A major problem to overcome is how to keep warm. You have probably noticed how cold you get even in a heated swimming pool. This is because the water takes your body heat away. People who spend a long time in cold water, such as divers and windsurfers, wear wet suits to keep themselves warm.

Many types of whale feed in the cold, polar seas and travel to warmer waters each year to give birth. Some of a mother whale's blubber is turned into milk to feed her calf. The baby whale must develop a thick layer of blubber in order to survive when it returns to colder water with its mother.

The weddell seal lives in the Antarctic, where temperatures on land may be colder than -20°C. The seal dives underneath the ice to escape from the winter gales. At such times it will be warmer in the water than on the land.

An otter's water-repellant fur helps to keep it warm both in the water and on land.

Mammals, such as whales and dolphins, that live in cold water have developed special body fat, called blubber. The blubber of a large whale may be up to 60 cms thick in some place. A blue whale weighs 193 tonnes. Just over a third of this weight may be its skin and blubber. Some types of whale migrate from their feeding grounds to warmer areas to breed. For several months of each year they do not eat, and their body fat turns into food.

Seals and sea lions also have blubber to protect them against the cold. Their bodies are covered in hair, because, unlike dolphins and whales, they spend some time on land. The otter, on the other hand, hardly has any blubber, and relies on its thick coat of fur to keep it warm.

Keeping warm, or cool

Humans can survive in cold climates because they live in heated homes and wear special clothes. In the winter we can wrap up warm against the cold. Explorers can even survive in the frozen polar regions, or in the freezing cold of space. We avoid overheating in the summer, or in hot climates, by wearing the right clothes. Light-coloured clothes are best when the sun is strong, because they reflect the heat. Dark-coloured clothes absorb heat.

Whatever the temperature of the air, our internal body temperature tends to remain around the same (about 37°C) unless we are ill.

This Arab boy is wearing clothes suitable for a hot climate. The long sleeves and headdress protect his skin from the sun's rays and the white material reflects the heat.

The body temperature of some animals depends entirely on the temperature of their surroundings, however. These are called cold-blooded animals and they include reptiles. First thing in the morning, a crocodile can only move quite slowly, but as its body takes in warmth from the sun and its blood warms up, it becomes more active and moves more quickly. When it gets too hot it will cool off in the water.

People who live in freezing climates have traditionally worn animal skins to keep themselves warm.

Some insects and spiders can actually survive the cold winter asleep because of a chemical in their blood that stops it from freezing. Fish that live in the cold polar seas survive in the same way. Many mammals escape the cold by hibernating – finding a warm dry place and going into a deep sleep that can last the whole of the winter.

If a chameleon wants to get warm it turns a dark colour to absorb the heat of the sun. If it becomes too hot, it turns a light colour to reflect the heat. This one is just beginning to turn a light green.

Hiding from danger

The large light-coloured spots on the dark back of this fawn look like the patterns of light and shade to be found in forests. It makes it less likely to be seen by predators.

The patterns and colours on the body of many types of animal are adapted to blend in with the animal's surroundings. The right colour and pattern can completely camouflage an animal. The sandy-brown fur of a lion helps it to stalk its prey across the sandy-brown earth and grass of the African plains. Animals that live in the Arctic, such as the polar bear and Arctic fox, are white so that they don't show up against the snow. The ptarmigan, a bird found in areas which are snow-covered only in winter, changes its feathers from brown in the summer to white in the winter.

This stick insect is so well camouflaged, it looks almost more stick-like than the stick!

Insects are particularly good at blending in with their surroundings. The many different kinds of stick insect are all adapted to look like the plants on which they feed. Some insects do very convincing imitations of twigs, leaves and tree bark. The looper caterpillar looks like a plant stem, while a bush cricket mimics a dead leaf. The umber moth is almost invisible on tree bark and the Chinese character moth looks like a distasteful bird dropping.

Some creatures take the business of camouflage a step further and actually change colour from moment to moment, depending on where they are. The chameleon is the best-known of these. It can change from green to brown in a matter of minutes, as it moves from a leaf to a tree trunk. Flatfish and octopus can change the colour of their body to match the sea-bed by expanding and contracting special skin cells that allow different colours to appear.

This Brazilian butterfly mimics a dead leaf, including imitation spots of black and white mould.

A leaf-frog, almost completely hidden on the forest floor.

Showing off

The silver-coloured fur of this mountain gorilla shows that he is the leader of his group.

▼ The magnificent male bird of paradise displays his tail feathers to attract a female.

Many animals use their body coverings for display, to send signals to other animals. The hairs on the back of a dog's neck will stick up when it is angry, and the hairs on a a cat's tail do the same. Monkeys raise and lower their eyebrows to communicate anger and alarm to other monkeys.

Many birds, normally the males, have developed brightly coloured feathers. These are used both to attract a female and to frighten off competitors. Females are usually a dull colour so that they blend in with their surroundings when sitting on their nest. Parrots may stick up their head feathers to form a threatening display.

This traditional clown make-up makes the child's eyes, lips and cheeks look much bigger than they really are. When worn by a real clown, in a circus ring, the make-up enables the clown's face and expressions to be seen even from the back row of seats.

▼ *A Masai warrior in traditional dress, with a painted skin originally intended to frighten the enemy.*

The colour of our skin reddens when we are embarrassed, hot or angry, but we have no control over this. We are unable to change the colour of our skin in a natural way. Instead, people all over the world paint their bodies and faces. The way in which they do this varies, and depends on what is considered 'beautiful' or 'fierce' in the society in which they live.

Skin change

Throughout our lives we shed thousands of tiny dead skin cells, which are replaced by new ones. Some animals shed a whole layer of skin at one time. Snakes and lizards shed their skin in this way and underneath is a new, shiny skin.

Birds moult their feathers a few at a time, so that they always have enough to fly with and to keep them warm. Mammals moult their fur or hair at certain times of the year. A thick coat of fur that has kept an animal warm all winter will not be needed in the summer. If you have a pet dog or cat, you will notice when it moults because it will leave hairs all over the furniture.

An American corn snake, shedding its skin. When a snake needs to renew its skin a lubricating liquid is released under the skin. This separates the old skin from the new skin underneath, turning the old skin cloudy – even where it covers the snake's eyes. The snake, unable to see properly, will hide away for up to a week until the skin is ready to be shed. The snake then wriggles out of its old skin in a matter of minutes.

When animals are moulting they tend to look rather scruffy.

Most insects, including butterflies and dragonflies, change their shape several times before they become adults. These changes are called metamorphoses.

This dragonfly has just climbed out of its old, nymphal, skin (which it is leaving behind still clinging to a stalk) and has now changed into an adult dragonfly.

Crabs have to shed their old armoured shell so that they can grow. They swell their bodies with water, which splits the old shell. The crab then climbs out of its armour. The skin underneath is soft, so it must hide away from danger until the shell hardens. Locusts, woodlice and spiders also shed their tough skin as they grow.

29

Glossary

Absorb Take in water or heat.

Algae Very small plants that grow in water but have no stems, roots or leaves.

Ancestors Relatives who lived a long time ago.

Bacteria Tiny living creatures that can cause infection or illness.

Blubber A thick layer of body fat in animals such as whales and seals that helps keep them warm.

Camouflage Being able to hide by having a body that is the same colour (or shape) as the surrounding area (grass, sand, etc).

Contract Get smaller or close up.

Expand Get larger or open up.

Hibernate Spend the winter in a deep sleep.

Lubricating liquid A slippery liquid, like an oil.

Migrate Journey between two areas (or countries) at certain times of the year, usually to avoid very bad weather or to find food.

Moult To shed body covering (such as skin, feathers or shell) so that it can be replaced by a new one.

Mucus A protective slime.

Predator An animal that kills other animals for food.

Prey An animal that is hunted for food.

Reflect Cause light and heat to bounce off.

Shed Get rid of.

Sweat A salty liquid that comes out of holes in the skin in hot weather to help cool the body down.

Books to read

Natures Secrets Series by Paul Bennett (Wayland Publishers Ltd, 1994)

The Body and How it Works by Steve Parker (Dorling Kindersley, 1987)

Science Facts: *Human Body* by Lionel Bender (Grange Books, 1992)

The Secret of Sciences: *Senses* by Robin Kerrod (Cherry Tree Books, 1991)

Further notes

The human body is completely covered in skin, which protects the internal organs from the surrounding environment. It protects us from internal injury, the sun's harmful rays and infection from bacteria. Our skin helps us to control our body temperature and acts as a sensory organ, giving us a sense of touch and enabling us to detect cold, heat and pain.

Keeping warm or cool

Blood capillaries near the surface of the skin can help prevent the body from becoming too hot. The capillaries widen, allowing more hot blood to flow near the skin's surface and therefore more heat to be lost. When it is cold the capillaries become smaller, reducing the amount of blood that flows near the surface and the amount of heat lost. Although the outer skin temperature may vary greatly, the internal body temperature of a healthy person stays fairly constant at between 35.8°C and 37.7°C.

Sweating also helps to cool our body temperature. When our body temperature rises, the sweat glands absorb water from the surrounding capillaries. The water collects in the glands and eventually travels up the sweat duct and on to the skin. As the sweat evaporates, it takes heat from the body and helps to cool it down.

Parts of the human skin

Epidermis – Tough outer layer of skin cells which forms a protective layer. The surface of our skin is made up of dead skin cells.

Dermis – This layer contains blood vessels, sweat glands and nerves with sensors to detect heat, cold, pain and touch.

Follicle – The hole in the skin out of which a hair grows.

Malpighian layer – This layer produces skin pigment that protects us against the sun's rays.

Sensory nerves – Separate sensory nerves can detect cold, pain, heat and touch.

Blood capillaries – These bring oxygen and food to the skin and remove carbon dioxide. The capillaries close to the surface of the skin help to control body temperature.

Sweat glands – These produce sweat (salty water) that passes on to the surface of the skin through a pore (hole) when the body is hot.

Erector muscles – These make hairs on the skin stand up.

Fat layer – This is a food store that can be broken down by the body and used if necessary. It also forms an insulating layer to reduce the heat lost from the body.

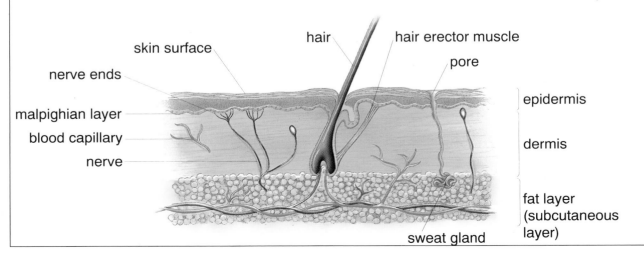

Index